CONQUER ADVERSITY

Strengthen Mental Grit, Defeat Obstacles, Elevate Your Inner Resilience, and Achieve Victory Over Life's Hardships

PREM SAGAR SUNCHU

YOUR FREE GIFT !!

As a token of my thanks for taking out time to read my book, I would like to offer you a **Free-Gift**:

Click the Below Link and Download your **Free eBook PDF**.

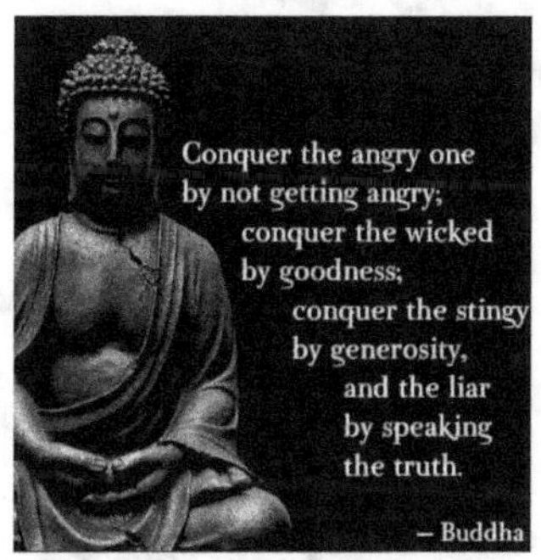

"The Power of Community: Thriving Together"

ABOUT THE AUTHOR

Prem Sagar Sunchu, the Accomplished Author of "Conquer Adversity"

Meet **Mr. Prem Sagar**, an ordinary soul born in the vibrant city of Secunderabad, India, where the tapestry of life weaves stories of resilience and dreams. His journey is a testament to the power of perpetual learning, where every encounter is a lesson, and every moment holds the potential for growth.

A man of many dimensions, Mr. Sagar embodies the qualities of a perpetual student, a dedicated listener, and a dreamer who gazes at the stars but keeps his feet firmly grounded. His aspirations soar high, and his relentless pursuit of them is fueled by a genuine desire to make a positive impact on those around him.

Having served as a Chief Manager in the prestigious State Bank of India, Mr. Sagar brings a wealth of experience from the world of banking. However, for him, retirement isn't a conclusion but a commencement—a reminder that life's true journey begins when one can reflect on the wisdom gained from the first innings.

In Mr. Sagar's view, retirement is not a retreat but a stepping stone to a realm of infinite possibilities. It's an opportunity to surpass the ordinary, where the canvas of life awaits new brushstrokes of creativity and purpose. For him, the "be good and do good policy" isn't just a mantra; it's a guiding principle that shapes his approach to life.

As he embraces the second innings, Mr. Sagar encourages others to view retirement not as a winding down but as a springboard to new endeavors. It's a time when accumulated wisdom meets fresh energy, and the monotony of routine gives way to the vibrancy of creativity. His belief is clear: retirement is not just a number; it's a chapter where the richness of experience meets the possibilities in abundance.

In the world of Mr. Prem Sagar, retirement is not a period of rest but a canvas waiting to be painted with the colors of newfound wisdom, creativity, and a different outlook on life.

Prem Sagar Sunchu
M.Com, LLM, Certified Independent Director (IICA)
GOI,
Author, Sole Arbitrator and Legal Consultant, Free-
lancer

ACKNOWLEDGEMENTS

In profound gratitude, I extend heartfelt appreciation to my amazing parents. To my caring and resilient mother, **Smt. S.L. Lakshmi**, who gracefully navigated the challenges of my father's service transfers, made countless sacrifices to bind our family together. My father, **Shri S.R. Lakshman Rao**, stands as my enduring role model—his post-retirement vibrancy, marked by a dedicated hobby of reading and writing, serves as the very foundation that propels me into the realm of authorship. A debt of gratitude is owed to my beautiful wife, **Smt. S.P. Padma Sree** is a constant source of inspiration, unwavering strength, and invaluable guidance. Balancing family responsibilities and the intricate path of an author, her presence has been the foundation of my journey.

To my handsome sons, **S.P. Gautam Sagar**, **S.P. Prayag Sagar**, and **S.P. Akshaj Sagar**, whose unwavering support and responsibility bear testament to the great strength they provide. Their motivation fuels my endeavors across all the diverse traits I undertake.

I owe thanks to **Mr. Som Bathla**, an **Amazon #1 Best-selling** author, for his mentorship, motivation, and guidance in the realms of **Writing, Self-Publishing, and Launching Books**. His support has been instrumental in initiating my journey as an Authorpreneur.

My Sincere thanks to **Mr. Sooraj Achar**, who is also an Amazon Bestselling Author, for his **Professional Editing,** Formatting, and Publishing support.

In acknowledging these pillars of support, I am reminded that the tapestry of my life and authorial pursuit is woven with threads of love, sacrifice, and inspiration. With profound thanks to my family, who stand as my bedrock of strength and motivation.

DEDICATION

To the guiding stars of my universe—my Parents, Grandparents, Parents-in-law, Brothers, Sisters, the cherished members of our extended Family and Friends. Their unwavering support and boundless encouragement have been the driving force behind my Author Journey.

In the tapestry of my life, each of them has woven threads of inspiration and resilience, transforming mere words into stories and dreams into realities. Their confidence in me has been a constant source of strength, propelling me forward through the path of this journey.

With heartfelt gratitude, I dedicate the pages of my work to the pillars of love and encouragement that they are, recognizing that every word I pen is a tribute to the collective spirit of our family. May this dedication reflect the depth of my appreciation for the profound impact they have had on my creative journey.

"Conquer Adversity" is my fourth book in the series of five books-"**The Resilient Mind.**"

UNLOCK THE POWER WITHIN

"Unlock the Power Within: Forge Unshakable Re-silience, Defy Life's Challenges, and Rise Victori-ous Over Every Obstacle."

My Book will help you navigate life's toughest moments by tapping into your inner strength.

CONTENTS

INTRODUCTION: HARNESSING THE POWER OF ADVERSITY

"Adversity introduces a man to himself." – Albert Einstein

Introduction

Life presents us with challenges that can feel overwhelming, leaving us with a choice: to succumb or to rise above. It is often in the face of adversity that we learn the most about ourselves and our abilities. Adversity, though uncomfortable, serves as a powerful catalyst for personal growth. Whether it's losing a job, facing health issues, or enduring emotional struggles, hardships push us to tap into our hidden reserves of strength. This chapter dives into the nature of adversity, why it's inevitable, and how it holds the key to unlocking resilience and personal mastery.

1.1 The Inevitable Struggle: Understanding Adversity as a Universal Experience

Adversity is one of life's few guarantees. Every person, regardless of background, social status, or achievements, will face difficulties. Yet, while the form of these challenges varies—financial, emotional, physical, or relational—the experience of adversity remains a common thread that unites humanity. According to a study conducted by the American Psychological Association (APA), over 60% of adults report having experienced at least one major traumatic event in their lives. What sets people apart is not whether they face adversity, but how they choose to respond to it.

The inevitability of struggle doesn't mean that we should fear it. Rather, understanding that adversity is part of the human condition allows us to reframe these experiences. Instead of viewing challenges as threats, we can start to see them as opportunities for growth. This mindset shift is crucial to mastering adversity.

Case Study 1: J.K. Rowling's Journey from Poverty to Success

J.K. Rowling, author of the Harry Potter series, offers a powerful example of how adversity can fuel personal growth. Before achieving worldwide success, Rowling was a single mother living on government assistance. She struggled with depression, financial instability, and the loss of her mother. At her lowest point, she contemplated giving up on writing entirely. Yet, it was during this period of immense difficulty that she began penning the stories that would later captivate millions.

Rowling has openly spoken about how her hardships shaped her resilience and creativity. In her commencement speech at Harvard, she remarked, "Failure meant a stripping away of the inessential. I stopped pretending to myself that I was anything other than what I was and began to direct all my energy into finishing the only work that mattered to me." Rowling's story illustrates how adversity can serve as a transformative force, paving the way for greater success and self-awareness.

1.2 The Gift of Resilience: How Challenges Shape Character

Resilience, the ability to bounce back from adversity, is not something we are born with—it is cultivated through experience. When we face difficulties, our capacity to adapt and recover strengthens. This process of developing resilience, often referred to as "post-traumatic growth," was explored by researchers Tedeschi and Calhoun in the 1990s. They found that individuals who endured significant adversity often experienced increased personal strength, enhanced relationships, and a greater appreciation for life.

Resilience is built through continuous engagement with challenges. It's not about avoiding hardship but about embracing the struggle and using it as a stepping stone to personal development. Every setback provides an opportunity to learn, adapt, and grow stronger.

Case Study 2: Nelson Mandela's 27 Years in Prison

Nelson Mandela's life offers one of the most striking examples of how adversity can shape resilience. Sentenced to life in prison for his activism against apartheid in South Africa, Mandela spent 27 years behind bars, enduring harsh conditions and isolation. Many people in his position might have become bitter, but Mandela emerged with an even greater sense of purpose and inner strength.

He once said, "Do not judge me by my successes, judge me by how many times I fell down and got back up again." Mandela's resilience not only transformed him personally, but it also empowered him to lead South Africa through a peaceful transition from apartheid to democracy. His time in prison became the crucible that forged his character, enabling him to forgive those who oppressed him and work toward reconciliation.

Research on resilience supports Mandela's story. A study published in the journal *Psychological Science* found that individuals who experienced moderate adversity were better equipped to handle future stress and challenges compared to those who faced either no adversity or extreme hardship. This research underscores the idea that overcoming difficulties fosters resilience, equipping us to handle life's future obstacles with greater confidence.

1.3 From Setbacks to Success: The Roadmap to Personal Mastery

The path from adversity to success is not linear, but it is navigable. It requires shifting the way we perceive setbacks, understanding that they are not dead ends but detours that offer valuable lessons. The key to mastering adversity lies in viewing it as a training ground for personal growth.

One critical step in this journey is adopting a growth mindset—a term coined by psychologist Carol Dweck. A growth mindset is the belief that abilities and intelligence can be developed through effort and perseverance. People with a growth mindset see challenges as opportunities to learn rather than threats to their self-worth. They embrace effort, understand that failure is part of the process, and persist despite setbacks.

Another essential component of mastering adversity is emotional resilience. As life throws curveballs, maintaining emotional balance becomes vital. Techniques such as mindfulness, self-compassion, and cognitive reframing help individuals manage their emotions in difficult times. A Harvard study on emotional regulation found that individuals who practice mindfulness and cognitive reframing are better equipped to handle stress and bounce back from adversity.

Building a support system is another important step on this journey. Research shows that social support buffers the negative effects of stress. Surrounding oneself with people who offer encouragement and guidance during tough times can make all the difference in how one navigates hardship. As we'll explore in future chapters, resilience is not only an individual trait but also one that is nurtured through relationships and community.

Finally, mastering adversity requires a forward-looking vision. Instead of getting stuck in the pain of the moment, those who successfully navigate hardships keep their eyes on the long-term goal. They use their struggles as fuel for future success, continuously learning, adapting, and evolving.

Conclusion: Embracing the Journey of Growth

Adversity is an inevitable part of life, but it holds within it the potential for tremendous personal growth. Whether we are facing financial struggles, emotional pain, or professional setbacks, how we respond to these challenges determines the course of our lives. Through cultivating resilience, shifting our mindset, and building strong support systems, we can transform adversity into the very thing that propels us toward success.

The power to master adversity lies within each of us. As this book continues, you'll gain deeper insights into practical tools, case studies, and proven strategies to build resilience and thrive, no matter what life throws your way. The journey may be difficult, but the rewards of personal mastery, mental grit, and inner strength are well worth it.

Resources:

1. American Psychological Association. (2020). *Resilience in a time of crisis: An update.* Retrieved from APA.org.

2. Tedeschi, R. G., & Calhoun, L. G. (1996). *The post-traumatic growth inventory: Measuring the positive legacy of trauma.* Journal of Traumatic Stress, 9(3), 455–471.

3. Dweck, C. S. (2006). *Mindset: The new psychology of success.* Random House.

4. Harvard Medical School. (2020). *Mindfulness practices for emotional resilience.* Retrieved from <u>Harvard.edu</u>.

5. Psychological Science. (2013). *The benefits of experiencing moderate adversity: Psychological and physical resilience in adulthood.* 24(5), 761–768.

Chapter 1

THE GRIT FACTOR: BUILDING UNSHAKABLE MENTAL STRENGTH

"Success is not final, failure is not fatal: It is the courage to continue that counts." – Winston Churchill

Introduction

Mental strength is often viewed as an abstract concept, but it's one of the most tangible factors influencing success. While talent and intelligence play a role in achievements, they pale in comparison to the power of grit. Grit—defined as a combination of perseverance and passion for long-term goals—allows individuals to push past obstacles, endure discomfort, and keep going when the path is rough. This chapter explores the concept of grit, its role in overcoming life's difficulties, and the practical strategies to cultivate mental resilience. Through research, case studies, and real-life examples, we'll uncover how anyone can build unshakable mental strength.

1.1 The Psychology of Grit: Why Mental Fortitude Matters More Than Talent

Grit is more than just perseverance; it's the deep-seated belief that effort, sustained over time, leads to mastery. Psychologist Angela Duckworth, a leading researcher on grit, defines it as "the passion and perseverance for long-term goals." In her groundbreaking research, Duckworth found that grit is a better predictor of success than intelligence, talent, or social skills. People with high levels of grit tend to achieve more, not because they are naturally gifted, but because they refuse to quit.

One of Duckworth's studies followed cadets at West Point Military Academy, where only the toughest individuals survive the rigorous training. Surprisingly, the most successful cadets weren't those with the highest IQs or physical strength.

Instead, they were the ones who demonstrated grit—the ability to push through hardship and stay committed to their long-term goals despite challenges. This finding highlights a crucial point: talent may get you started, but grit is what keeps you going.

Case Study 1: The Determination of Thomas Edison

Thomas Edison's journey toward inventing the light bulb is one of the most well-known examples of grit in action. Despite over a thousand failed attempts, Edison famously said, "I have not failed. I've just found 10,000 ways that won't work." His relentless pursuit of his goal eventually revolutionized modern life. Edison's grit—his ability to persist in the face of repeated failures—was key to his success. He didn't rely solely on his intelligence or inventiveness; rather, it was his refusal to give up that made him a pioneer in his field.

Scientific research backs up this idea. A study published in the *Journal of Personality and Social Psychology* found that individuals who scored high on measures of grit were significantly more likely to achieve long-term success compared to those with lower scores, even when controlling for intelligence. The conclusion is clear: while talent can provide a head start, it's grit that ensures you cross the finish line.

1.2 Cultivating a Resilient Mindset: Practical Tools to Strengthen Your Inner Self

Building mental strength requires more than just persistence—it involves a range of practical tools that can be honed over time. The first key to developing grit is self-discipline, the ability to delay gratification and stay focused on long-term goals. Research conducted by psychologist Roy Baumeister demonstrated that self-discipline predicts success more accurately than IQ. His study showed that people who can resist short-term temptations are more likely to achieve their long-term goals, whether in academics, work, or personal development.

In addition to self-discipline, emotional regulation plays a critical role in developing mental toughness. Learning to manage your emotions in difficult situations—whether through mindfulness, cognitive behavioral techniques, or stress-reduction strategies—helps build resilience. A study published in *Emotion* found that individuals who practiced mindfulness techniques had greater emotional stability and were better able to cope with adversity.

Finally, determination—the unrelenting drive to achieve despite setbacks—is the fuel that keeps mental toughness alive. Determination is not a fixed trait but a muscle that strengthens with use. By consistently challenging yourself to push beyond your comfort zone, you build the mental stamina required to handle life's inevitable difficulties.

Case Study 2: Serena Williams' Road to Tennis Greatness

Serena Williams is one of the most successful athletes in history, and her career offers a powerful example of grit. Despite facing racial discrimination, injuries, and personal setbacks—including life-threatening health complications—Serena never lost sight of her goals. Her discipline, determination, and emotional control are key elements of her success. In interviews, Williams has emphasized the importance of mental strength in overcoming both physical and emotional barriers. "You have to believe in yourself when no one else does," she once said. Her journey exemplifies how mental grit can elevate performance, even when faced with overwhelming odds.

1.3 Overcoming the Fear of Failure: Reframing Setbacks as Stepping Stones

One of the most significant barriers to developing mental toughness is the fear of failure. Many people view failure as a sign of weakness or incompetence, but this perspective is not only limiting—it's inaccurate. Failure is an essential part of the growth process. In fact, the most successful people are often those who have failed the most, as they have learned from their mistakes and used those lessons to improve.

Reframing failure as a learning opportunity rather than a defeat can radically shift one's mindset. Carol Dweck, a psychologist known for her work on mindset, emphasizes the power of viewing challenges as chances for growth. Those with a "growth mindset" believe that abilities and intelligence can be developed through effort and learning, whereas those with a "fixed mindset" see failure as a permanent reflection of their limitations. Shifting from a fixed to a growth mindset allows individuals to see setbacks as part of the journey to mastery rather than an endpoint.

To overcome the fear of failure, it's essential to adopt strategies that turn mistakes into valuable lessons. One approach is to practice self-compassion—recognizing that failure is part of the human experience and doesn't define one's worth. Research by Kristin Neff has shown that individuals who practice self-compassion are more resilient and better able to bounce back from failures than those who are overly self-critical.

1.4 The Power of Perseverance: Staying the Course During Life's Toughest Moments

Grit is ultimately about perseverance. It's the ability to keep going when everything in you wants to quit. Life's most difficult moments often feel insurmountable, but history is filled with examples of individuals who persisted through extreme adversity to achieve extraordinary success.

Perseverance is not just about pushing through for the sake of endurance; it's about maintaining focus on the end goal, even when progress feels slow. This mindset was highlighted in a *Psychological Science* study, which found that people who stayed committed to their goals during periods of high stress experienced greater long-term success and personal satisfaction.

Case Study 3: The Grit of Malala Yousafzai

Malala Yousafzai, a Pakistani activist for female education, displayed remarkable perseverance in the face of extreme adversity. After being shot by the Taliban for advocating girls' education, Malala could have given up her fight. Instead, she emerged stronger, continuing her activism on a global scale. In 2014, she became the youngest-ever recipient of the Nobel Peace Prize. Her perseverance in the face of violence and oppression has inspired millions, demonstrating that grit can overcome even the most daunting obstacles.

Her story is supported by research on the power of perseverance. Studies have found that individuals who maintain long-term focus and commitment, despite difficulties, are more likely to achieve their goals and experience personal fulfillment. Malala's grit was not born overnight; it was built over years of dedication and resilience in the face of constant threats.

Conclusion: Grit—The True Key to Success

Mental strength, or grit, is a skill that anyone can develop. It is not limited to the naturally talented or the highly intelligent; rather, it's cultivated through persistence, self-discipline, emotional regulation, and perseverance. The stories of Thomas Edison, Serena Williams, and Malala Yousafzai illustrate how grit can help us push through failure, overcome obstacles, and achieve extraordinary success.

As we navigate life's challenges, it's essential to remember that setbacks are not the end—they are part of the journey. By reframing failures as opportunities for growth and staying focused on long-term goals, we can build the unshakable mental strength needed to face adversity head-on and come out victorious.

Resources:

1. Duckworth, A. L., Peterson, C., Matthews, M. D., & Kelly, D. R. (2007). *Grit: Perseverance and passion for long-term goals.* Journal of Personality and Social Psychology, 92(6), 1087–1101.

2. Baumeister, R. F., & Tierney, J. (2011). *Willpower:*

Rediscovering the greatest human strength. Penguin Press.

3. Dweck, C. S. (2006). *Mindset: The new psychology of success.* Random House.

4. Neff, K. (2011). *Self-compassion: The proven power of being kind to yourself.* William Morrow.

5. Psychological Science (2013). *The power of perseverance: Goal commitment and success under stress.*

CHAPTER 2

THRIVING UNDER PRESSURE: MASTERING EMOTIONAL RESILIENCE

"The oak fought the wind and was broken, the willow bent when it must and survived." – Robert Jordan

Introduction

Life's challenges come in waves, sometimes bringing unexpected hardships that can shake our emotional foundation. Whether it's navigating professional pressures, personal loss, or the steady weight of daily stress, we are often left feeling overwhelmed. But emotional resilience—the ability to adapt and recover in the face of adversity—can be developed.

In this chapter, we'll explore how to thrive under pressure by managing stress, restoring energy, cultivating emotional intelligence, and embracing mindfulness practices. Through science-backed techniques and real-life stories, you'll gain practical strategies for mastering emotional resilience and turning adversity into growth.

2.1 The Emotional Rollercoaster: Managing Stress and Anxiety During Hardship

Stress and anxiety are inevitable parts of life, especially in difficult situations. In fact, the body's stress response is a natural mechanism designed to protect us, increasing alertness and focus during immediate threats. However, prolonged stress can erode mental and physical well-being. Research published by the American Psychological Association reveals that chronic stress is associated with various health issues, including cardiovascular disease, depression, and impaired cognitive function (APA, 2019).

Case Study 1: Olivia's Unexpected Career Crisis

Olivia, a 34-year-old marketing professional, had always been highly regarded for her performance. But when her company restructured, Olivia found herself taking on multiple roles, each with increasing demands. As the workload intensified, so did her anxiety. She began experiencing sleepless nights, a racing heart, and frequent emotional outbursts.

Olivia sought counseling, where she learned cognitive behavioral techniques to identify stress triggers and modify her reactions. She also incorporated breathing exercises to ground herself in overwhelming moments. Through consistent practice, Olivia reduced her anxiety and developed the emotional capacity to handle her heightened responsibilities.

Key Takeaways: Stress and anxiety are normal reactions to challenges, but they don't have to control your life. Learning to identify triggers and using tools like cognitive reframing and grounding techniques can significantly reduce the emotional burden.

2.2 Bouncing Back from Burnout: Techniques for Restoring Energy and Focus

Burnout is a state of emotional, physical, and mental exhaustion caused by prolonged stress. It depletes energy, clouds focus, and can even lead to a sense of disillusionment with life. According to the World Health Organization (WHO), burnout has become a global health concern, affecting millions of individuals in both personal and professional settings (WHO, 2019). Burnout manifests not only as exhaustion but also in cynicism and feelings of inefficacy.

Case Study 2: David's Path to Recovery

David, a 42-year-old high school teacher, began his career with enthusiasm, spending long hours developing lesson plans and connecting with students. But after years of over-commitment and ignoring his own needs, David hit a wall. He struggled with fatigue, headaches, and lost his passion for teaching.

David's recovery began with setting boundaries at work, ensuring that he didn't overextend himself. He reintroduced self-care routines, such as weekly hikes and mindfulness journaling, to recharge mentally and physically. Slowly, he rediscovered his focus and love for teaching.

Key Takeaways: Burnout doesn't happen overnight, and recovery requires intentional self-care. Setting healthy boundaries, taking breaks, and engaging in restorative activities like exercise and hobbies are vital to replenishing energy and avoiding complete burnout.

2.3 Harnessing Emotional Intelligence: Turning Adversity into Emotional Growth

Emotional intelligence (EQ) is the ability to recognize, understand, and manage our own emotions while also being attuned to the emotions of others. Research by psychologist Daniel Goleman emphasizes that individuals with high emotional intelligence are better equipped to handle stress, communicate effectively, and turn adversity into opportunities for growth (Goleman, 1995).

Developing self-awareness, self-regulation, and empathy plays a crucial role in emotional resilience. Self-awareness allows us to recognize emotional triggers before they spiral out of control. Self-regulation helps in managing reactions in the face of frustration, anger, or sadness. Empathy, the ability to understand the feelings of others, fosters stronger relationships and emotional support systems, which are key during challenging times.

How to Build EQ for Emotional Resilience:

- **Self-awareness:** Practice regular self-reflection, journal your thoughts, and notice emotional patterns in different situations.

- **Self-regulation:** Pause before reacting emotionally. Take deep breaths or count to ten when you feel triggered.

- **Empathy:** Practice active listening with others, acknowledging their emotions without judgment.

2.4 Finding Peace Amidst the Storm: Meditation, Mindfulness, and Other Grounding Practices

In times of stress and emotional overwhelm, finding inner calm can feel impossible. However, mindfulness practices such as meditation, breathing exercises, and body scans have been proven to regulate the stress response and improve emotional stability. A study conducted by Harvard Medical School showed that regular meditation can reduce the brain's "fight-or-flight" response, leading to decreased stress and anxiety (Harvard Health Publishing, 2018).

Mindfulness Practices for Emotional Resilience:

- **Meditation:** Spend 10–15 minutes daily in focused meditation. Sit in a quiet space, close your eyes, and focus on your breath. When your mind wanders, gently bring it back to your breath.

- **Body Scanning:** Lie down comfortably and slowly direct your attention to each part of your body, from head to toe, noticing areas of tension and consciously releasing it.

- **Breathing Exercises:** Try the 4-7-8 breathing technique to calm anxiety: inhale for 4 seconds, hold for 7 seconds, and exhale for 8 seconds. Repeat several times.

Conclusion

Emotional resilience isn't something we are born with, but a skill we develop over time. By learning to manage stress and anxiety, recognizing and recovering from burnout, cultivating emotional intelligence, and using mindfulness practices, you can not only survive but thrive under pressure. With each challenge you face, your resilience grows, transforming adversity into an opportunity for emotional growth. The key is to be patient with yourself, practice self-care, and seek support when needed.

Resources

- American Psychological Association (2019). The impact of stress. Retrieved from [www.apa.org]

- Goleman, D. (1995). *Emotional Intelligence: Why It Can Matter More Than IQ*. Bantam Books.

- Harvard Health Publishing (2018). The Science of Meditation: A new study investigates how it helps reduce stress. Retrieved from [www.health.harvard.edu]

- World Health Organization (2019). Burn-out an "occupational phenomenon."

CHAPTER 3

FROM SETBACK TO COMEBACK: REINVENTING YOURSELF AFTER FAILURE

"Success is not final, failure is not fatal: it is the courage to continue that counts." – Winston Churchill

Introduction

Failure is a universal experience, but it's what comes after that defines who we are. Setbacks, whether in our personal or professional lives, can leave us feeling defeated and unsure of our next steps. However, the journey from failure to success often leads to profound personal transformation. Reinventing oneself after adversity isn't just about bouncing back—it's about growing stronger and more resilient. In this chapter, we'll explore how to turn life's lows into powerful opportunities for change, reflect on past lessons, and build a new foundation for a brighter future. By drawing from real-life stories and evidence-based strategies, this guide will show you how to rise after you fall.

3.1 The Art of Reinvention: Turning Life's Lows into Personal Transformation

When faced with failure, many people feel as though they've hit a wall. But failure is not the end; it's a pivot point. Psychologist Carol Dweck's research on *growth mindset* highlights that people who view challenges as learning opportunities are more likely to succeed in the long run (Dweck, 2006). Reinvention begins when we stop seeing failure as something to fear and start recognizing it as a springboard for transformation.

Case Study 1: Sarah's Career Reinvention

Sarah was a successful corporate executive until a failed merger left her without a job. At 45, she found herself questioning her future. After a few months of self-reflection, Sarah realized she had always been passionate about writing. Using her business experience, she launched a career as a business writer and consultant. What began as a setback turned into an opportunity for her to pursue something more aligned with her interests. Today, Sarah is a published author and speaks at events, sharing her journey of career reinvention.

Key Takeaway: Reinventing yourself after a setback means taking control of the narrative. By focusing on personal growth and learning from the experience, you can chart a new path forward, one that may align more closely with your true passions.

3.2 The Role of Reflection: Learning from the Past to Shape the Future

Reflection is a crucial step in the process of transformation. Without understanding what went wrong, it's difficult to know how to move forward. Reflection allows you to take a deeper look at the setback, identify patterns, and uncover valuable insights. Research shows that people who regularly reflect on their experiences are more likely to make thoughtful decisions and avoid repeating the same mistakes (Schön, 1983).

Reflection Exercises for Personal Growth:

- **Journaling:** Writing down your thoughts can help clarify your feelings. Take 10 minutes daily to jot down your reflections on the setback. Focus on what you've learned and how you can apply those lessons moving forward.

- **Questions to Ask Yourself:** What went wrong? What could I have done differently? What strengths did I rely on during the challenge? How can I use those strengths going forward?

Case Study 2: John's Financial Setback

John was a small business owner whose company faced bankruptcy after a series of poor financial decisions. Instead of giving up, John took time to reflect on the mistakes that led to his business's failure. He sought mentorship, enrolled in financial management courses, and developed a deeper understanding of entrepreneurship. Three years later, John started a new company that thrived—thanks to the lessons he learned from his previous failure.

Key Takeaway: Failure offers valuable lessons, but only if you take the time to reflect on it. Reflection transforms painful experiences into meaningful insights, giving you a clearer perspective on how to approach future challenges.

3.3 Building a Stronger Foundation: Creating New Habits and Routines Post-Adversity

Once you've reflected on your setbacks and learned from them, it's time to rebuild. This process often involves developing new habits and routines that align with the version of yourself you're striving to become. According to research from Charles Duhigg in *The Power of Habit*, it takes about 21 days to form a new habit, but it requires consistency and intention (Duhigg, 2012).

Steps to Create New Habits:

1. **Identify One Key Area of Focus:** Choose one area—whether it's health, career, or personal development—that you want to improve.

2. **Start Small:** Break your goal into manageable steps. If you're trying to improve your fitness, start with

10-minute daily exercises rather than aiming for hour-long workouts right away.

3. **Use Habit Triggers:** Associate your new habit with an existing routine. For example, drink a glass of water every morning right after brushing your teeth.

4. **Track Your Progress:** Use a habit-tracking app or a simple calendar to mark off each day you complete the habit.

Building Resilience Through Routine:

After his business failure, John (from our earlier case study) used structured routines to rebuild his life. He set specific financial goals, practiced daily journaling, and maintained a consistent workout routine to keep his mind and body sharp. This structured approach helped him stay focused, manage stress, and maintain the discipline needed to succeed in his new venture.

Key Takeaway: New habits create the foundation for long-term success after a setback. By establishing consistent routines, you strengthen your resilience and prepare yourself for future opportunities.

3.4 Real-Life Examples: Stories of Triumph After Major Failures

History is full of people who have turned devastating failures into extraordinary comebacks. These stories are not just inspiring but demonstrate the power of persistence and reinvention.

Thomas Edison's Tenacity:

Thomas Edison, one of the most famous inventors of all time, faced countless failures in his attempts to create the electric light bulb. When asked about his many unsuccessful attempts, he reportedly said, "I have not failed. I've just found 10,000 ways that won't work." Edison's resilience and refusal to give up eventually led to one of the most groundbreaking inventions in history.

J.K. Rowling's Rise After Rejection:

Before J.K. Rowling became one of the world's best-selling authors, she was a struggling single mother living on welfare. Her manuscript for *Harry Potter* was rejected by 12 different publishers. However, she didn't give up on her dream of becoming an author. Eventually, her persistence paid off when a small publishing house took a chance on her work. Today, Rowling's story is a testament to the power of perseverance in the face of failure.

Key Takeaway: Major setbacks can lead to extraordinary comebacks. Whether it's Edison's endless experiments or Rowling's publishing rejections, the common thread is resilience. With determination and a willingness to keep pushing forward, anyone can turn failure into success.

Conclusion

Setbacks are not final. They are moments of opportunity that force us to pause, reflect, and grow. By learning from the past, building new habits, and embracing the process of reinvention, we can turn failure into a catalyst for personal transformation. Whether it's in your career, relationships, or personal development, the power to reinvent yourself is within your control. As history and countless personal stories have shown, failure is simply a step on the path to a stronger, more resilient you.

Resources

- Dweck, C. S. (2006). *Mindset: The New Psychology of Success.* Random House.

- Schön, D. A. (1983). *The Reflective Practitioner: How Professionals Think in Action.* Basic Books.

- Duhigg, C. (2012). *The Power of Habit: Why We Do What We Do in Life and Business.* Random House.

Chapter 4

THE POWER OF PERSPECTIVE: SHIFTING YOUR MINDSET DURING HARDSHIP

"The greatest discovery of my generation is that a human being can alter his life by altering his attitudes." – William James

Introduction

Hardship is an unavoidable part of life, but the way we respond to it is what shapes our future. While some may feel overwhelmed by adversity, others use it as a stepping stone to growth and personal development. The key difference lies in perspective. Shifting your mindset during tough times can open the door to resilience, learning, and emotional strength. This chapter explores how embracing a growth mindset, reframing negative thoughts, practicing gratitude, and owning your personal narrative can transform your experience of hardship into an opportunity for growth.

4.1 The Growth Mindset: How to Turn Challenges into Learning Opportunities

The concept of a *growth mindset*, introduced by psychologist Carol Dweck, is the belief that our abilities and intelligence can be developed through dedication and hard work (Dweck, 2006). People with a growth mindset see challenges not as threats, but as opportunities to learn and improve. This mindset helps individuals adapt to adversity by focusing on progress rather than perfection. In contrast, those with a *fixed mindset* may avoid challenges for fear of failure, viewing setbacks as confirmation of their limitations.

Case Study 1: Michael Jordan's Resilience

Consider Michael Jordan, widely regarded as one of the greatest basketball players in history. Early in his career, Jordan was cut from his high school basketball team. Many would have viewed this as a devastating failure, but Jordan used it as fuel to improve. He dedicated himself to honing his skills and eventually became a six-time NBA champion. Jordan's growth mindset—his belief in his ability to improve through hard work—allowed him to turn this early setback into a stepping stone to greatness.

Key Takeaway: By adopting a growth mindset, you can transform challenges into learning experiences. Hardship becomes a stepping stone to progress, pushing you to develop new skills and improve your resilience. You don't have to be perfect; you just have to keep moving forward.

Developing a Growth Mindset:

- **Embrace challenges:** View difficult situations as opportunities to learn.

- **Persist in the face of setbacks:** Understand that failure is a natural part of the growth process.

- **Learn from criticism:** Use feedback to improve rather than seeing it as a personal attack.

- **Celebrate small wins:** Recognize and celebrate progress, no matter how small, to keep motivation high.

4.2 Reframing Negative Thoughts: How to Change the Internal Dialogue During Tough Times

When we face hardship, it's easy to fall into a cycle of negative thinking. Thoughts like "I can't do this" or "I'm a failure" can dominate our internal dialogue, making it difficult to move forward. However, research from cognitive-behavioral therapy (CBT) shows that changing our thoughts can change our emotions and behavior (Beck, 1979). Reframing negative thoughts into more balanced, empowering ones is a powerful tool during tough times.

Steps to Reframe Negative Thoughts:

1. **Recognize the negative thought:** Pay attention to your internal dialogue. What limiting beliefs are driving your emotions?

2. **Challenge the thought:** Ask yourself, "Is this thought based on fact, or is it an emotional response?"

3. **Replace it with a positive alternative:** Find a thought that is more constructive. For example, replace "I'll never get through this" with "This is hard, but I can take it one step at a time."

Case Study 2: Emma's Mental Health Journey

Emma, a young professional, struggled with anxiety after losing her job during an economic downturn. Her internal dialogue was dominated by thoughts like "I'm not good enough" and "I'll never find another job." These thoughts worsened her anxiety and paralyzed her from taking action. Through therapy and self-reflection, Emma learned to recognize these negative patterns. She began practicing reframing techniques, changing "I'm not good enough" to "I'm facing a tough situation, but I have valuable skills." Over time, her anxiety reduced, and she regained confidence in her job search. Emma eventually found a new position that aligned with her goals and passions.

Key Takeaway: Reframing negative thoughts allows you to change your perspective and regain control over your emotions. By shifting your internal dialogue, you can reduce anxiety and approach adversity with a clearer, more empowered mindset.

4.3 The Role of Gratitude: Finding the Silver Lining in Adversity

Gratitude has been shown to significantly improve emotional well-being, particularly during difficult times. Research by psychologist Robert Emmons found that practicing gratitude can increase happiness, reduce depression, and improve overall mental health (Emmons & McCullough, 2003). When we actively look for things to be grateful for, even in the midst of hardship, we train our brain to focus on the positives rather than dwelling on the negatives.

Gratitude Practices for Tough Times:

- **Gratitude journaling:** Each day, write down three things you are grateful for, no matter how small. This shifts your focus to the positives in your life.

- **Gratitude reflection:** Take a few moments at the end of each day to reflect on a difficult situation and find one silver lining.

- **Gratitude letters:** Write a letter to someone who has positively impacted your life, expressing your appreciation.

Case Study: Viktor Frankl's Search for Meaning

Viktor Frankl, a psychiatrist and Holocaust survivor, exemplified the power of gratitude and meaning in the face of unimaginable adversity. In his book *Man's Search for Meaning*, Frankl described how even in the dire conditions of concentration camps, he found purpose and gratitude by focusing on small moments of beauty, kindness, or connection. His perspective allowed him to survive the physical and psychological hardships, teaching us that even in the darkest times, there is something to be grateful for.

Key Takeaway: Gratitude shifts your focus from what you've lost to what you still have. By cultivating gratitude, you can change how you experience hardship, making even the toughest challenges more bearable.

4.4 Changing the Narrative: Taking Control of Your Story in the Face of Hardship

One of the most powerful tools for overcoming hardship is the ability to take control of your personal narrative. Instead of seeing yourself as a victim of circumstances, you can view yourself as the hero of your own story. Changing your narrative means reframing your experience in a way that emphasizes growth, resilience, and personal agency.

How to Change Your Narrative:

1. **Identify the current narrative:** Are you telling yourself a story of failure, helplessness, or victimhood?

2. **Rewrite your story:** Start viewing your setbacks as challenges that shaped who you are today. Use language that empowers you—"I survived," "I learned," "I grew stronger."

3. **Live by your new story:** Once you've rewritten your narrative, start acting in alignment with it. Make decisions and take actions that reflect the ver-

sion of yourself you're becoming.

Example: Oprah Winfrey's Narrative of Triumph

Oprah Winfrey is one of the most influential people in the world today, but her early life was marked by hardship. Born into poverty and suffering abuse as a child, Oprah could have let these circumstances define her. Instead, she reframed her narrative. Rather than viewing herself as a victim, Oprah saw herself as someone with the power to overcome. She worked tirelessly to build her career and used her platform to inspire others with similar stories. Oprah's success is not just about fame or fortune—it's about the way she took control of her narrative and chose to see herself as a hero.

Key Takeaway: Changing your narrative gives you the power to turn your life's challenges into sources of strength. By rewriting your story, you shift from victim to victor, allowing you to approach hardship with resilience and determination.

ConclusionHardship is inevitable, but how we respond to it defines our journey. By adopting a growth mindset, reframing negative thoughts, practicing gratitude, and taking control of our personal narrative, we can shift our perspective and transform adversity into opportunity. These tools empower us to not only survive tough times but to thrive in their wake. Life's challenges don't have to hold us back—they can propel us forward into a stronger, more resilient version of ourselves.

Resources

- Beck, A. T. (1979). *Cognitive Therapy and the Emotional Disorders.* Penguin Books.

- Dweck, C. S. (2006). *Mindset: The New Psychology of Success.* Random House.

- Emmons, R. A., & McCullough, M. F. (2003). Counting blessings versus burdens: An experimental investigation of gratitude and subjective well-being in daily life. *Journal of Personality and Social Psychology, 84*(2), 377–389.

- Frankl, V. E. (2006). *Man's Search for Meaning.* Beacon Press. (Original work published 1946)

CHAPTER 5

BUILDING AN UNBREAKABLE SUPPORT SYSTEM: RELATIONSHIPS IN TIMES OF ADVERSITY

"Surround yourself with only people who are going to lift you higher." – Oprah Winfrey

Introduction

In times of hardship, having a strong support system can make the difference between feeling overwhelmed and finding the strength to keep going. While self-reliance is important, the connections we build with others provide us with emotional and practical resources that can ease our burdens. This chapter explores the value of a solid support network during adversity, the importance of asking for help, the role of vulnerability in deepening connections, and the need to build a circle of resilience through positive influences. Strengthening these relationships not only helps us navigate tough times but also fosters long-term emotional resilience.

5.1 The Importance of Connection: How a Strong Support Network Eases the Burden

A robust support system is a vital resource in times of stress or adversity. Research has repeatedly shown that individuals with strong social connections tend to experience better physical and mental health outcomes. According to a study published in *The American Journal of Psychiatry*, social support has been linked to lower levels of depression, anxiety, and stress (Cohen, 2004). This is because relationships act as a buffer, providing emotional comfort and practical assistance that can make difficult situations more manageable.

Support systems can take many forms: family members, close friends, colleagues, mentors, or even support groups. Each type of relationship offers something unique, whether it's a listening ear, guidance, or a sense of belonging. By nurturing these relationships, we create a safety net that cushions the impact of life's hardships.

Case Study 1: Sarah's Support Through Illness

Sarah, a single mother diagnosed with breast cancer, was initially overwhelmed by fear and uncertainty. However, her strong network of friends and family became her greatest asset. Her best friend, Lisa, accompanied her to every chemotherapy session, while her sister helped care for her children. The emotional and practical support provided by her community helped Sarah cope with the physical and mental challenges of treatment. With their help, she felt empowered to face her illness, rather than isolated by it.

Key Takeaway: Connection reduces feelings of isolation and provides a sense of shared burden. By fostering close relationships, you create a support system that can offer practical help, emotional encouragement, and a reminder that you're not alone.

Tips for Strengthening Relationships:

- **Regularly check in** with loved ones, even when things are going well. This builds a foundation of trust.

- **Offer help before it's asked for**; small acts of kindness can deepen bonds.

- **Practice active listening** to show you value their thoughts and emotions.

5.2 Asking for Help: Breaking the Stigma Around Seeking Support

Many people hesitate to ask for help because they fear being seen as weak, incapable, or a burden. However, seeking support is not a sign of weakness—it is a sign of strength and self-awareness. Studies have shown that individuals who seek social support during times of crisis tend to have better outcomes than those who try to manage everything on their own (Taylor et al., 2000). Yet, societal stigmas surrounding vulnerability often prevent people from reaching out when they need help the most.

Breaking this stigma starts with changing our mindset. Asking for help allows us to share our load and opens the door for others to support us in meaningful ways. It also creates opportunities for deeper connections, as people who care about us often want to help but don't know how unless we let them in.

Case Study 2: John's Journey to Asking for Support

John, a high-achieving professional, had always prided himself on his independence. When his business started struggling during a recession, he tried to shoulder the burden alone. The stress soon led to burnout, and he found himself on the edge of a breakdown. One day, after much internal struggle, he confided in a trusted mentor. To his surprise, his mentor didn't judge him but instead shared stories of his own challenges. By asking for help, John received valuable advice and emotional support that helped him navigate the business downturn, and he learned that vulnerability was not a sign of failure, but an avenue for growth.

Key Takeaway: Asking for help is not a weakness; it is a courageous act of self-care. By reaching out to others, you allow them to support you, which in turn can reduce your emotional and mental load.

Practical Advice for Asking for Help:

- **Be clear about what you need**: Whether it's advice, a listening ear, or practical assistance, clarity helps others know how to best support you.

- **Choose the right person**: Reach out to someone you trust who has the capacity to help.

- **Express gratitude**: Acknowledge the help you receive. It strengthens the bond and shows appreciation for the other person's effort.

5.3 The Power of Vulnerability: Strengthening Bonds Through Honest Communication

Vulnerability often feels risky, but it's one of the most powerful ways to deepen connections with others. According to research by Dr. Brené Brown, vulnerability is the birthplace of connection and courage (Brown, 2010). By opening up about our struggles, we invite others into our inner world, which fosters trust and intimacy.

Being vulnerable is not about oversharing or unloading all of your burdens at once. It's about being honest about how you feel and allowing others to see you as you are. This kind of communication encourages empathy and understanding and can create a strong emotional bond between people.

Why Vulnerability Strengthens Relationships:

- **It builds trust**: When you are open about your struggles, it encourages others to trust you and to open up in return.

- **It fosters empathy**: Vulnerability allows others to understand your experiences on a deeper level.

- **It promotes authenticity**: Being vulnerable helps you show up authentically, which strengthens the quality of your relationships.

Case Study: Laura's Healing Through Vulnerability

Laura had always been the rock for her family and friends. But after losing her job and experiencing depression, she felt unable to share her struggles, fearing she would be seen as weak. However, during a conversation with her closest friend, Laura broke down and opened up about her feelings. Instead of being judged, her friend offered her compassion and understanding. This moment of vulnerability brought them closer, and Laura felt more supported and less alone in her journey.

Key Takeaway: Vulnerability is a powerful tool for connection. By sharing your struggles, you invite others into a deeper relationship, which can provide both emotional relief and stronger social bonds.

5.4 Building a Circle of Resilience: Surrounding Yourself with Positive Influences

The people you surround yourself with have a significant impact on how you cope with adversity. Research shows that having a positive and encouraging social environment can improve resilience and overall well-being (Seeman, 1996). This means that the quality of your relationships matters just as much as the quantity. While it's important to have a wide support network, it's equally crucial to ensure that your inner circle is filled with people who uplift, inspire, and encourage your growth.

Sometimes, we need to evaluate our relationships and determine whether certain individuals are contributing to our resilience or hindering it. It's not about cutting ties indiscriminately, but about ensuring that the people closest to you are those who motivate and support your journey.

Steps to Build a Resilient Circle:

1. **Identify positive influences**: Who in your life makes you feel stronger, more capable, and supported?

2. **Distance from negativity**: Recognize individuals who consistently bring negativity or drain your energy, and consider limiting interactions with them.

3. **Foster new connections**: Seek out relationships with people who share your values, goals, and outlook on life.

Example: Building a Resilient Inner Circle

Mark, a young entrepreneur, found that some of his friends were constantly negative about his business ventures. They doubted his abilities and discouraged him from taking risks. Mark realized that this negativity was weighing him down. He made a conscious effort to spend more time with mentors and fellow entrepreneurs who believed in his vision and encouraged him to pursue his goals. Surrounding himself with positive influences not only improved his mindset but also led to greater success in his business.

Key Takeaway: Surrounding yourself with positive, encouraging individuals builds emotional resilience. These relationships create an environment where you feel supported, motivated, and capable of overcoming challenges.

Conclusion

Building an unbreakable support system is essential during times of adversity. Whether it's leaning on family, friends, or mentors, having a strong network can ease the emotional burden of difficult situations. By asking for help, embracing vulnerability, and surrounding yourself with positive influences, you create a circle of resilience that supports you in your darkest moments. Relationships aren't just sources of comfort—they are key to enduring, growing, and thriving through hardship.

Resources

- Brown, B. (2010). *The Gifts of Imperfection: Let Go*

of Who You Think You're Supposed to Be and Embrace Who You Are. Hazelden Publishing.

- Cohen, S. (2004). Social relationships and health. *American Psychologist, 59*(8), 676-684.

- Seeman, T. E. (1996). Social ties and health: The benefits of social integration. *Annals of Epidemiology, 6*(5), 442-451.

- Taylor, S. E., et al. (2000). Biobehavioral responses to stress in females: Tend-and-befriend, not fight-or-flight. *Psychological Review, 107*(3), 411-429.

CHAPTER 6

THE LONG-TERM VISION: MASTERING RESILIENCE FOR LIFELONG SUCCESS

"Out of adversity comes opportunity." — Benjamin Franklin

Introduction

Adversity is an inevitable part of life. How we navigate it not only shapes our present circumstances but also defines our future. While many see adversity as a momentary struggle, it holds the potential to be a long-term source of strength if approached with the right mindset. Mastering resilience is not about simply surviving difficult times but transforming those challenges into catalysts for personal and professional growth. In this chapter, we'll explore how adversity can become a foundation for lifelong success, and we'll examine strategies for building resilience that lasts beyond individual hardships.

6.1 The Journey of Adversity Mastery: From Short-Term Struggles to Long-Term Strength

"What lies behind us and what lies before us are tiny matters compared to what lies within us." — Ralph Waldo Emerson

Adversity often comes in waves—sometimes in small, manageable doses and other times in overwhelming tides. Yet, each challenge offers an opportunity for growth, and mastering these struggles is a journey that spans a lifetime.

In the short term, adversity pushes us to adapt, forcing us to hone our problem-solving skills and cultivate emotional endurance. These immediate reactions lay the groundwork for long-term strength. The key lies in reframing hardship not as a roadblock but as a stepping stone toward something greater.

Take the case of Sarah, a young entrepreneur who faced the collapse of her startup just six months after its launch. In the aftermath, Sarah could have given up on her dreams. Instead, she chose to reflect on her mistakes, sought mentorship, and invested time in learning new skills. Five years later, Sarah launched a new venture that not only succeeded but also became a model of resilience in her industry. Her short-term failure became the cornerstone of her long-term success.

Scientific Insight: Research published in the *Journal of Positive Psychology* supports the idea that individuals who experience early setbacks develop better emotional regulation skills, which contribute to long-term resilience. These individuals learn to manage stress and are more likely to succeed in future endeavors by building on their past experiences.

6.2 Building Legacy Strength: How to Develop Resilience That Endures

Resilience is often thought of as a personal trait, but it can be much more. It's something that can be cultivated, strengthened, and passed on. Legacy strength refers to the type of resilience that not only sustains you through personal hardships but also empowers others around you—be it family, friends, or even colleagues.

Developing enduring resilience requires intentional effort. It means nurturing a mindset that sees challenges as opportunities for growth, actively practicing self-compassion, and fostering strong connections with others. Importantly, legacy strength is not just about bouncing back but about growing stronger after each fall.

Case Study: John, a high school teacher, faced a health crisis that forced him to take time off work. During his recovery, John could have fallen into despair, but he focused on the bigger picture—his long-term legacy as an educator. He spent time mentoring younger teachers, sharing his journey of recovery, and inspiring them with the strength he had built through adversity. When he returned to the classroom, he wasn't just the same teacher; he was a pillar of resilience for his students and colleagues alike.

By focusing on legacy strength, you can transform your personal growth into something that benefits the community around you. Resilience, when cultivated and shared, has a ripple effect that can positively impact those around you for generations.

6.3 Adversity as a Teacher: Life Lessons That Shape Character and Success

"Adversity is the first path to truth." — Lord Byron

One of the greatest gifts adversity offers is the life lessons that come with it. These lessons, often hard-earned, shape not only our character but also our approach to future challenges. The experience of overcoming adversity teaches us patience, humility, and tenacity—traits that are essential for long-term success.

Adversity teaches us to be adaptable, to accept that things don't always go according to plan, and to find strength in the face of uncertainty. It also fosters empathy, as we become more understanding of the struggles of others, having faced our own.

In Sarah's case, her early entrepreneurial failure taught her the importance of resilience, but it also taught her how to be more compassionate toward others in her network who faced similar challenges. She learned to value collaboration over competition and built a support system that was instrumental in her later success.

Scientific Insight: A study published in *Psychological Science* highlights that individuals who face significant adversity are more likely to develop higher levels of empathy and social awareness. This shift in perspective can lead to improved interpersonal relationships and, ultimately, greater life satisfaction.

6.4 Preparing for the Future: Strategies for Continuous Growth and Adversity Management

Adversity will continue to show up throughout life, but we can prepare ourselves for it by actively developing strategies for continuous personal growth. Just as athletes train to improve their physical endurance, we must train our minds and emotions to handle future challenges.

Here are some actionable strategies to build and maintain resilience:

1. **Mindfulness Practice**: Regular mindfulness meditation can help improve emotional regulation, re-

duce stress, and enhance clarity during challenging times.

2. **Physical Health**: Maintaining physical health through regular exercise and proper nutrition strengthens your body and mind, enabling you to handle stress better.

3. **Reflective Journaling**: Writing about your experiences with adversity can help you gain perspective, recognize patterns, and identify lessons that will guide you in the future.

4. **Strengthen Your Support Network**: Surround yourself with positive, encouraging people who will stand by you in times of need. A strong support system provides emotional backing that makes overcoming adversity easier.

5. **Lifelong Learning**: Stay curious and invest in continuous learning. The more skills and knowledge you acquire, the better equipped you'll be to adapt to change and overcome obstacles.

Scientific Insight: According to a study published in *Health Psychology*, individuals who engage in regular resilience-building practices—such as physical activity and mindfulness—are more likely to recover quickly from stressors and maintain a positive outlook over time.

Conclusion

Mastering resilience is a lifelong process, one that transforms short-term struggles into lasting strengths. Through intentional effort, you can build a legacy of resilience that not only sustains you but also uplifts those around you. Adversity, when faced with courage and an open mind, becomes a powerful teacher that shapes our character and fuels long-term success. By embracing continuous growth, cultivating strong support systems, and adopting proven resilience-building strategies, we can prepare ourselves to face any challenge the future holds.

Resources

1. *Journal of Positive Psychology* – Studies on emotional regulation and resilience.

2. *Psychological Science* – Research on empathy and so-

cial awareness.

3. *Health Psychology* – The role of physical activity and mindfulness in stress management.

4. Brown, B. (2012). *Daring Greatly: How the Courage to Be Vulnerable Transforms the Way We Live, Love, Parent, and Lead.* Penguin Books.

5. Seligman, M. E. P. (2011). *Flourish: A Visionary New Understanding of Happiness and Well-being.* Free Press.

CONCLUSION: TRIUMPH OVER LIFE'S CHALLENGES

"Strength does not come from winning. Your struggles develop your strengths. When you go through hardships and decide not to surrender, that is strength." — Arnold Schwarzenegger

7.1 Reflecting on the Journey: Recap of Key Lessons on Adversity Mastery

Life is unpredictable, often filled with challenges that test our strength, character, and resilience. Throughout this book, we've explored various facets of adversity and how to navigate them with grace, determination, and emotional resilience. Let's take a moment to reflect on the key lessons we've uncovered along the way.

Grit Matters: The ability to persevere through difficult times is not only a predictor of success but also of long-term well-being. Grit, the combination of passion and perseverance, enables us to push through temporary hardships to achieve lasting growth. Research by psychologist Angela Duckworth shows that grit is often a stronger predictor of success than talent alone. It's not about avoiding challenges but about developing the inner resolve to persist through them.

Emotional Resilience: As we've discussed, emotional resilience—the capacity to adapt and recover from stress—is crucial in overcoming adversity. Life's hardships often come with emotional turbulence, but learning how to regulate these emotions, reframe negative thoughts, and seek social support helps to ensure that we emerge from difficulties stronger. Studies in the *American Journal of Psychiatry* emphasize that emotionally resilient individuals experience lower levels of stress and are more likely to view setbacks as temporary rather than permanent.

Mindset Shifts: We explored how a growth mindset—the belief that abilities and intelligence can be developed—can transform our experience of adversity. Instead of viewing failures as the end of the road, a growth mindset encourages us to see them as learning opportunities. As Carol Dweck's research has shown, individuals with a growth mindset are better equipped to overcome obstacles because they focus on improvement and personal development rather than immediate success.

Supportive Relationships: The importance of a strong support system cannot be overstated. Whether it's friends, family, or mentors, the people we surround ourselves with can either uplift us during tough times or drain our emotional resources. Case studies throughout this book have demonstrated the power of supportive relationships in adversity management. Psychologists have long found that social support is a protective factor against mental health struggles, particularly during times of crisis.

Each of these pillars—grit, emotional resilience, mindset, and relationships—has equipped us with the tools to navigate life's inevitable challenges. Together, they form the foundation for mastering adversity and turning hardships into opportunities for growth.

7.2 The Path Forward: Embracing Challenges as Opportunities for Growth

Life is not defined by the absence of adversity but by how we respond to it. When we approach challenges with the mindset that they are temporary obstacles rather than permanent roadblocks, we change the way we experience difficulty. This shift in perspective allows us to move from a place of resistance to one of growth.

Consider the story of Maria, a corporate executive who lost her job during an economic downturn. Rather than viewing this as a failure, Maria saw it as a chance to reassess her career. She pursued further education, rebranded herself, and eventually landed a more fulfilling role in a different industry. Maria's ability to turn a seemingly devastating event into a new opportunity is a prime example of growth through adversity.

The path forward, therefore, is not to avoid challenges but to embrace them as a natural part of life's progression. Each challenge offers lessons, and each hardship presents a chance to grow stronger. This mindset, rooted in the belief that every setback is a stepping stone, allows us to lead lives filled with purpose and resilience.

Scientific Insight: Research from the *Journal of Personality and Social Psychology* supports the notion that individuals who adopt a positive reframing strategy during times of adversity report higher levels of personal growth. This ability to see the silver lining, even in difficult situations, fosters a long-term growth mindset that can benefit all areas of life.

Adversity is not a threat—it's an invitation. It invites us to dig deeper, discover strengths we didn't know we had, and become more resilient in the face of future challenges. By shifting our focus from fear of failure to excitement for growth, we can transform even the most difficult circumstances into opportunities for personal evolution.

7.3 A Final Word on Resilience: Becoming the Master of Your Own Destiny

Throughout this journey, one thing has become clear: resilience is not a passive quality, but an active process. It's the conscious choice to rise after each fall, to seek out growth even when the road seems uncertain, and to believe in your capacity to triumph over life's challenges. Mastering resilience is about more than just survival—it's about thriving despite adversity and creating a life defined by purpose and strength.

Case Study: Consider the story of David, a small business owner who faced bankruptcy after a market crash. Instead of succumbing to despair, David rebuilt his business from the ground up, adopting new strategies and seeking guidance from mentors. His resilience not only saved his business but led him to mentor other entrepreneurs facing similar struggles. Today, David is a beacon of resilience, having turned his adversity into a legacy of helping others navigate their own challenges.

David's story exemplifies a key truth: resilience is not just about bouncing back; it's about bouncing forward. It's the proccss of emerging from hardship with a greater sense of purpose, strength, and determination to achieve long-term success.

As we conclude, it's important to remember that every individual has the capacity to shape their own destiny. Resilience is the tool that allows us to steer through life's storms with confidence and clarity. You are not at the mercy of life's challenges; rather, you are the architect of your own future. By cultivating grit, emotional resilience, a growth mindset, and supportive relationships, you become the master of your own destiny.

Empowering Thought: Scientific research published in *Psychological Science* shows that individuals who believe in their ability to influence their own outcomes (a trait known as *locus of control*) are more resilient in the face of adversity. They are also more likely to experience long-term success and personal fulfillment.

Your story is still being written. Each chapter, filled with its own set of challenges and triumphs, adds to the richness of your life's narrative. No matter where you are on this journey, know that resilience is your greatest asset. It will not only carry you through life's hardest moments but will also em-power you to build a future filled with strength, purpose, and fulfillment.

Conclusion

Mastering adversity is not a destination but a journey—a journey marked by personal growth, resilience, and an unwavering belief in the power to overcome life's challenges. We've recapped the essential lessons of grit, emotional resilience, mindset shifts, and the value of supportive relationships. The path forward calls on you to embrace each challenge as an opportunity for growth. With resilience, you can shape your own destiny, becoming stronger, wiser, and more equipped to face whatever lies ahead.

Remember, adversity is not the end—it's the beginning of something greater.

Resources

1. Duckworth, A. L. (2016). *Grit: The Power of Passion and Perseverance*. Scribner.

2. Dweck, C. (2006). *Mindset: The New Psychology of Success*. Random House.

3. *Journal of Personality and Social Psychology* – Studies on personal growth through adversity.

4. *American Journal of Psychiatry* – Research on emotional resilience and stress management.

5. Seligman, M. E. P. (2011). *Flourish: A Visionary New Understanding of Happiness and Well-being*. Free Press.

MAY I ASK YOU FOR A SMALL FAVOR?

I want to express my sincere gratitude for choosing to invest your time in reading this book. Your decision to explore this work among countless others means a lot to me.

I hope that within these pages, you've discovered actionable insights that can enhance your daily life. Your journey doesn't have to end here, though.

May I kindly request an additional 30 seconds of your valuable time?

Sharing your thoughts about the book through a review would be immensely appreciated. Your review serves as a beacon, guiding other readers to take a chance on my books. It's a small gesture that carries significant weight in the world of authors.

To submit your review effortlessly, please click on the link below. It will take you directly to the book's review page:

"Conquer Adversity"

Alternatively, you can also find the "**Reviews Section**" of this book's page on Amazon.

Your review will require just a minute of your time but will make a monumental difference in helping me connect with a broader audience and I eagerly look forward to reading your review.

Once again, thank you for your unwavering support of my work.

DISCLAIMER

This book is for educational purposes only. Readers acknowledge that the author does not render legal, financial, medical, or professional advice. The content within this book has been derived from various sources. Please consult a licensed professional before attempting any techniques outlined in this book.

By reading this document, the reader agrees that under no circumstances is the author responsible for any direct or indirect losses incurred as a result of the use of the information contained within this document, including but not limited to errors, omissions, or inaccuracies.

Adherence to all applicable laws and regulations, including international, federal, state, and local governing professional licensing, business practices, advertising, and all other jurisdictions, is the sole responsibility of the purchaser or reader.

Neither the author nor the publisher assumes any responsibility or liability whatsoever on behalf of the purchaser or reader of these materials. Any perceived slight of any individual or organization is purely unintentional.

www.ingramcontent.com/pod-product-compliance
Lightning Source LLC
Chambersburg PA
CBHW061722250726
48657CB00002B/724